THE AMAZING LIFE CYCLE OF PLANTS

All inquiries should be addressed to:
Barron's Educational Series, Inc.
250 Wireless Boulevard
Hauppauge, NY 11788
www.barronseduc.com

ISBN: 978-1-4380-5043-0

Library of Congress Control Number:
2017958534

Date of Manufacture: February 2018
Manufactured by: WKT Co., Ltd.,
Shenzhen, China

Printed in China
9 8 7 6 5 4 3 2 1

THE AMAZING LIFE CYCLE OF PLANTS

Written by
Kay Barnham

Illustrated by
Maddie Frost

BARRON'S

Look around you. How many plants and flowers
and trees and grasses can you see?
These natural beauties grow over and over again.
But how do they do it?

Get ready to dig deep and find
out more about the amazing
life cycle of a plant…

A seed is a baby plant. It is wrapped in a shell to keep it safe until it is time to grow.

There are lots of different types of seeds.
Avocado stones, apple seeds, and acorns are all seeds.

For a seed to grow, everything must be just right. There must be enough water, heat, and light, as well as the right type of soil.

When the seed cracks open,
roots grow down and a shoot
grows up. This sunflower seed
has turned into a seedling!

The shoot grows taller and thicker.
Soon it becomes the plant's stem.

The stem is strong enough to support the plant
as it grows bigger and more leaves appear.
It also carries water and food from the roots.
These will help the plant grow.

The plant's leaves are very important. They take in a gas called carbon dioxide. When this gas mixes with water and sunlight, it makes a sugary food for the plant.

Now the plant has energy to grow.

The leaves give out
another gas called
oxygen. Humans need
oxygen to survive.

Once the plant is fully grown, flowers appear. First, there is a bud. Slowly this opens to show the petals.

Flowers are bright and bold. They have a strong smell. This makes it easy for bees, butterflies, and other creatures to find them.

Deep inside the flower, there is a sweet liquid called nectar. Bees use this to make honey. Insects drink it to give them energy.

As they hunt for nectar, creatures carry pollen from flower to flower. Pollen also floats through the air in the wind. It is because of pollen that flowers make seeds.

It is important
that seeds do not fall
straight down. If they
land in the plant's shade,
seeds will not grow.

Instead, the plant scatters its seeds far and wide.
When seeds travel to many different places,
more of them might grow into new plants.

Seeds scatter in different ways. The wind might blow them away. Seeds might float on the tide. Sometimes, seedpods burst and fire their seeds outward.

Animals scatter seeds, too.
When they eat fruit, the seeds hidden
inside travel through the animals
and out the other end!

Did you know that some trees and plants need fire to survive? This giant redwood tree does not release seeds until there is a fire. The heat then makes the pinecones open.

Ash from the fire makes the soil the perfect place for a new tree to grow.

Plants such as ferns, mosses,
and algae do not grow seeds.
They grow tiny, round
spores instead.

The wind blows spores away from the plant. Some land in damp places and, if other spores land nearby, a brand new plant may start to grow.

A plant's life cycle is the time it takes to grow from seed to flower, scatter seeds, and die.

The life cycle of some plants takes just weeks. Others might live for a year.

The life cycle of the
Madagascar palm tree
is as long as 100 years!

The life cycles of plants are very important to farmers and gardeners. Farmers need to know when to sow crops and when they will be ready to harvest.

Gardeners need to know what
to plant so that their gardens are
colorful all year round!

THINGS TO DO

1. Grow your own sunflower! Plant the sunflower seed in soil and remember to water it. Then watch how tall it grows...

2. Collect as many different seeds as you can and stick them onto a wall chart. Remember to label each one!

3. Make a colorful word cloud! Start with "plant," then add any other words that this word makes you think of. Write them all down using different colored pens. Start like this...

ROOT PLANT SEED

NOTES FOR PARENTS AND TEACHERS

This series aims to encourage children to look at and wonder about different aspects of the world in which they live. Here are some specific ideas for getting more out of this book:

1. Suggest that children keep a plant diary. They could plant sunflower seeds and draw or take photos of the plants every day to see how they change and grow.

2. Ask children to decorate a paper plate to show the different stages of a plant's life. It could be any plant, from an oak tree to a pea. Spin the plate to show the plant's life cycle.

3. Put on a plant life cycle play! Ask children to pretend they are a seed growing into a plant, before seeds are dispersed and the life cycle starts all over again.

4. Make a collage of a plant's life cycle using seeds and cuttings from the plant itself.

5. Search online for a time-lapse video of a sunflower growing from a seed to a flower to show children.

PLANTS BOOKS TO SHARE

From Seed to Plant
by Gail Gibbons
(Holiday House, 1991)

National Geographic Readers: Seed to Plant
by Kristin Baird Rattini
(National Geographic Children's Books, 2014)

If You Plant a Seed
by Kadir Nelson
(Balzer & Bray, 2015)

Plants Can't Sit Still
by Rebecca E. Hirsch
(Millbrook Picture Books, 2016)

The Tiny Seed
by Eric Carle
(Puffin, 1997)